10 Promises of a Great Sports Parent

CRAIG L. MORRIS

WestBow Press books may be ordered through booksellers or by contacting:

WestBow Press
A Division of Thomas Nelson & Zondervan
1663 Liberty Drive
Bloomington, IN 47403
www.westbowpress.com
1 (866) 928-1240

ISBN: 978-1-9736-4632-7 (sc)
ISBN: 978-1-9736-4633-4 (e)

Library of Congress Control Number: 2018913812

Print information available on the last page.

WestBow Press rev. date: 12/13/2018

Contents

Introduction

"I can tell you are a good dad." Startled, not even knowing who the speaker was or who they were addressing, I turned around to see a man looking right at me. Our family was at a sandwich place and this stranger looked deeply into my eyes as if he wanted to communicate a message of vital importance. "I can tell by the way your daughter laughs with you that you are a great dad." These words of encouragement almost brought tears to my eyes. It is amazing how words from a stranger can penetrate into one's soul.

I sat with that "feel good" statement for a few moments, and then, reality crashed in on me when I thought, "What would he have concluded if he would have watched me on the sidelines of my child's game this past weekend?"

Tension filled my soul in this powerful moment. The collision of euphoric joy and crippling shame fueled a desire in me to move towards becoming an even better parent. For me, the battlefield is the Arena (this is the name I've given for the field, course, pool, court, gym, etc. – wherever your child competes). It is here where my dreams and demons collide in a toxic cocktail of emotions, thoughts, and far too often, behavior that misses the mark.

We all want to be great parents, great sports parents. Sometimes our own challenges impact us as we try to parent well. Whether they are wounds from the past, needs in the present, or fears for the future, we are often limited in our effectiveness and need help in setting a positive, hopeful course for our young athletes. *The 10 Promises of a GREAT Sports Parent* can help you move past some of the barriers and cross the finish line of raising a great child, and a great athlete!

The Power of a Promise

"But it is not only that I know myself in the mirror of my promises. My people, the ones who belong to me, who depend on me, also know me by the promises I have made. What I promise is what I am and will be to them. Only if they really know what I am can they live with me in trust. They know me in the important way, not by reading my analyst's notes, but by knowing my power to keep promises."

Lewis Smedes

Over the years, I have gathered hundreds of parents together in discussion forums to glean lessons from their best practices and their worst mistakes. I have interviewed dozens of *former elite athletes* to glean from their wisdom and learn from their experiences. I have spoken with *parents of elite athletes* at the top of their specialty in the Arena. Of the many lessons I have uncovered in my research, one has risen above the rest. <u>Healthy sports parents are on a course different from the mainstream</u>. They have set a distinct path with divergent goals and are moving through their parenting days with a unique and healthy operating system. They have identified a positive future and have made a covenant with themselves to do their part to help their child get there.

The journey of raising great kids and athletes begins with the power of a promise. Setting the right path for them to travel begins with a promise. We all know that promises are only as good as the character to keep the promise. We also know that promises have a dual payoff, benefitting both parents and the young athletes they are seeking to raise well. In short, a promise creates a new, healthy, and powerful story. When this positive story gets deeply implanted in the heart and soul of your athlete, much fruit will be produced.

You may be sitting there thinking, "Really? Why is a promise so important?" I'm glad you asked! Take the example of marriage. Have you ever been to a wedding where the bride and groom made a weak-kneed pledge like, "I will commit myself to you for as long as I am happy?" What do you think are the chances of this marriage being healthy and vibrant for years to come? What we promise significantly influences the result. Contrary to popular opinion, the promise contained in traditional marriage vows ("I will… 'til death do us part.") is not a declaration of present feelings, but is a proclamation of a future commitment. The same is true with sports parenting. A weak and wobbly-kneed promise to your young athlete will fail to provide them with the foundation and the framework required to help them live a flourishing life. Making a solid promise, the right content with the right heart, will set your young athlete up for success inside and outside of the Arena.

There is a saying in agriculture, *"The best time to plant a tree was 20 years ago. The second best time is now."* I would have loved to have been equipped with a different parenting operating system ten years ago when I first sauntered on the sidelines of my children's athletic careers. It may not have been "20 years ago," as the agriculture phrase asserts, but wouldn't it be a good idea to begin to become the healthy parent that will raise a great athlete – today? If not now, when are you going to begin to plant the seeds of success in the heart, soul, and mind of your young athlete? These promises won't guarantee that you will raise an elite athlete. These promises will encourage and equip you to set your child up for success both inside and outside of the Arena!

"When you make a promise, you tie yourself to another person by the unseen fibers of loyalty. You agree to stick with people you are stuck with. When

everything else tells them they can count on nothing, they count on you."

Lewis Smedes

Welcome to the 10 Promises of a GREAT Sports Parent!

1

I promise to remember that you are a child.

"So let them be little, 'cause they're only that way for a while."
Billy Dean

"I'm not paying for any pre-puberty private training!" The packed room full of overly competitive sports parents erupted with laughter. This wise and insightful mother was onto something–maybe we should remember that they are young?

One day when I was bemoaning the lackluster

performance from one of my young athletes, it dawned on me, "The biggest problem with my young athlete is that they are a kid!" Ten out of ten kids think like kids, feel like kids, and behave like kids. Kids have different operating systems than adults.

Here are a couple of uniquely beautiful and true things about your young athlete:

- *They move quickly from playing sports to being a kid again.* There seems to be a connection between age and how quickly young athletes get over disappointment. Seldom do kids stew over losses, playing time, or sports related disappointments. Kids walk into the Arena as kids and out of the Arena as kids. They never stop being kids, even if they "kill it," or "fall flat on their face." Wouldn't it be valuable to allow our athletes to just be kids instead of holding them hostage in our dark, adult world of wounds, needs and fears? What would you want at the end of a competition? Sometimes all a child wants is a smile from you and a big treat at the end of the game.

I never knew what was going on out in right field, all I knew is at the end of the game I'd get a free snow cone. I'd be out there, "Ahhh, free snow cone. Free snow cone." "Brian, what's the score?" "Free Snow cone! Free snow cone at the end of the game! If you play they're gonna give you a free snow cone. Even if you play half game you get the whole... you don't get a half snow cone, you get a whole snow cone for half the game. The people that play whole game get a whole snow cone and the people that play half game get a whole snow cone. So it's always whole. Always a whole snow cone. So, I'd rather play half game. I'd rather play half. Still get the whole snow cone..."

Brian Regan (Comedian)

– *Often, relationships are more important to your young athlete than the competition.* What do parents often hear when they ask the question, "What was the highlight of your game?" They will frequently offer a response like, "Hanging out with my friends." As we grow older, we become more small-minded, focusing primarily on the competition. We begin our sporting journey with relationships front and center as they should be, and then over time, pride, selfishness, and ego warps us and morphs what is most important. Isn't teaching your young athlete to be a good teammate, to encourage others, and to deal with victory as well as defeat in a respectful manner, a part of the life lessons we as parents should strive to teach our children?

"Then at one point in my career, something wonderful happened. I don't know why or how, but I came to understand what "team" meant… I learned I could impact the team in an incredible and consistent way. I learned I could impact my team by caring first and foremost about the team's success and not my own."
Don Mattingly

– *Your child's self-talk will be shaped by the words they hear from you following their training or competition.* Sports research indicates that a child's self-talk, the internal messages a child tells themselves, parrots the affirming or discouraging words they hear from the adults around them. The words we utter can enhance a child's belief in themselves and their courage to be who they are designed to be. The words you share with your child leaving the Arena are very important. Choose wisely!

"Once we believe in ourselves,
we can risk curiosity, wonder,
spontaneous delight, or any experience
that reveals the human spirit."
e.e. cummings

Your young athlete needs *YOU* to remember that they are a kid! Parents need to learn how to give their young athletes the special gift of time, space, and the blessing of just being accepted as a human being – and a kid! Regardless of your opinion of their performance, your post-Arena speech will leave an imprint on your child for years to come. If you want to set your child up for success, promise to allow them to be the child that they are!

"I've learned that people will forget
what you said, people will forget
what you did, but people will never
forget how you made them feel."
Maya Angelou

2

I promise to look for the good in you and your performance.

"Until you have formed the habit of looking for the good instead of the bad in others, you will be neither successful nor happy."
Napoleon Hill

"Did you see that train wreck out there today?" The father of the best player on our team shared a glimpse into his heart and mind in a solemn, and rare, moment of transparency. His daughter was, by far, the best player on our team. I was shocked. I had never seen his daughter have a bad game, including this one. In my dismay I shook my head and muttered a simple, "No."

"My daughter couldn't do anything right out there! She has a lot of work to do!" he blurted out in frustrated tones. Now what is most unsettling about that exchange is that I was thinking the exact same thing about my child! I was so disappointed to realize that I was so caught up in watching my young athlete, I missed many things. I missed the game. I missed the play of the other players. I missed the opportunity to connect with my wife and the other parents. And most importantly, I missed the opportunity to encourage and connect with my young athlete. As we look for the good rather than intensely searching for the bad parts in ourselves and others, we will increasingly feel truly alive and free to be the people we were designed to be.

It is vital that we as parents search diligently for the great choices and moments in our kid's character and performance. Here are a few suggestions that have flowed from my experiences and research to retrain our eyes and mind to have a vision for the good:

- *Change the hypothesis.* One of the best ways to change what you are looking for is to change the message that is driving it. Like a squirrel looking for nuts, the mind will look for evidence to support your assertions. If you believe that your child is lazy and unmotivated, what do you think you will find? If you believe your child is a hard worker, is it possible that you might see flickers of effort that you can encourage and fan into flame?

"What we see depends mainly
on what we are looking for."
John Lubbock

– *Get rid of the bad memories and hold on to the good ones.* One speaker eloquently shared a powerful truth about the manner in which we grasp the stories and events in our lives: "Memory is very treacherous about the best things…it treasures up the refuse of the past and permits priceless treasures to lie neglected" (Charles Spurgeon). Too true. We have the ability and responsibility to jettison the bad tapes in our minds, which tend to play over and over, and wisely, intentionally, and lovingly choose to focus on the good memories. In doing so, we will create the space for our young athlete to write a new, better story for their life, one without the shackles of their past plaguing them today.

"Let go. Why do you cling to pain?
There is nothing you can do about the
wrongs of yesterday. It is not yours to
judge. Why hold on to the very thing
which keeps you from hope and love?"
Leo Buscaglia

A sports parent came bemoaning the lack of effort from their child and their child's team. In fact, the lack of proper motivation represents a huge challenge for athletes and parents alike. I challenged this person to keep their mouth shut and their phone on their lap, taking notes of every positive thing that their child did. As time went on, I extended the challenge to include looking for the positive contributions that teammates were making. You know the rest of the story – this person became more encouraging, more positive, and happier. If you want to set your young athlete up for success – look for and encourage the good you both see and want to see in their lives!

"Any fool can walk in off the street and
tell you what's wrong with something.
It takes wisdom to discover what is right
and good about something."
Howard Hendricks

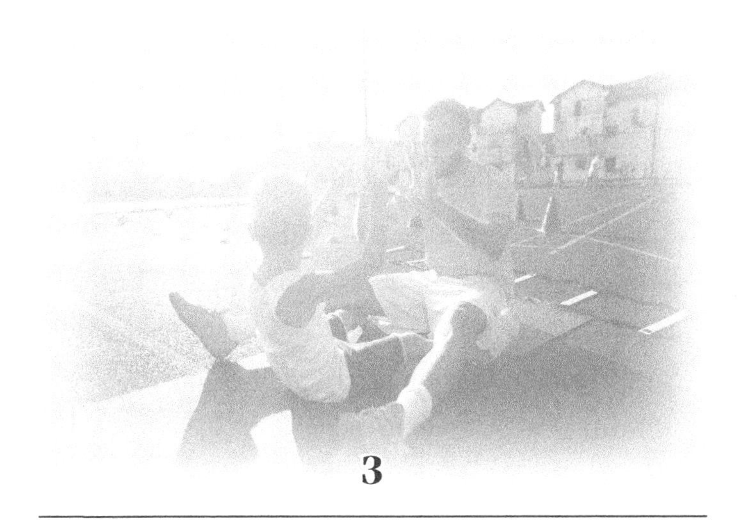

3

I promise to be the person I want you to be.

"The best thing you can do for your kids is be a good example."
John Wooden

"Remember when I told you a month ago to set some goals for yourself? I told you to write them down and put them in a place where you can see them everyday. Do you remember that conversation?" With a furrowed brow and raised eyebrows, my stern look was certainly sending a message of disappointment.

With her head held low, my daughter mumbled a simple word, "Yes."

"Did you do it?" I quickly and aggressively responded.

With a lingering, grace-pleading voice, she uttered two more words, "Not yet."

I shrugged my shoulders, looked deep into her eyes with a stern, disappointed look, spun around and abruptly exited the room. What type of impact do you think this very brief conversation may have had upon my young athlete? What indelible impression may have been imprinted upon her soul? Am I a horrible parent?

I took a few more steps away from my daughter's room and I heard a deep, inner voice within me, whispering to my soul with a strong and convincing tone, "Have *YOU* made a list of your goals yet? Have *YOU* written them down? Are *YOU* reviewing them daily?" Gulp. My mind quickly concluded, "I'm not living up to the standard I have created for my own child." In that moment I was reminded, once again, that the greatest lessons in life are caught – not taught. Still learning, I'm trying to speak less and live better. I'm trying to be the living example of who I want my kids to be.

Over the years I have coached my children and others in various sports, I have emphasized four athletic principles that we would do well as parents to apply to ourselves:

- *Focus.* There is a famous and funny scene in the movie *Up* where the attention of a dog is quickly diverted as he yells out, "Squirrel!" This word has become symbolic in our home when someone's attention is not where it should be. Distraction is a worthy opponent indeed. We've all witnessed moments during competition when a child missed a play because they were daydreaming, watching kids on the playground, or just not paying attention to the task at hand. Some athletes can be easily distracted. They need to learn how to focus, to acquire the ability to discipline their mind to shut out unhelpful distractions. In the same way, parents need to silence the distractions that can take them off of their mission to be an encouraging and supportive force in their child's life. What would it look like if we as parents were focused on the right priorities?

"Excellence is never an accident. It
is always the result of high intention,
sincere effort, and intelligent execution;
it represents the wise choice of many

alternatives – choice, not chance,
determines your destiny."
Aristotle

– *Have passion.* Philosophers and professors have long understood passion to be something that is, "a special fit between an activity and a person" (Geneviève Mageau). Passion can't be forced; it has to be found deep in one's heart. Regardless of the health of the force driving it, elite athletes have an incredible passion for excellence, improving, and winning. Likewise, we as parents of young athletes need to discover *the right passion about the right things.* We can't control our children, but we can serve them, lead them and love them with passion. Wouldn't our young athlete be better served if we were as *passionate* about growing their character as we are in developing them athletically?

"Nothing great in the world has been
accomplished without passion."
Georg Hegel

– *Work hard.* Research indicates that what your athlete believes about themselves and how they are encouraged will either put a ceiling over their head or a sling-shot around their bum. Carol Dweck in *Mindset* explains that if your young athlete has heard and believes that they are "talented," eventually they will take shortcuts and give up earlier than they should. But, if they believe that hard work is the key component towards fruitfulness and success, those who choose to put in the effort will be rewarded handsomely for their character! Perhaps our young athletes will be inspired to train hard through their long practices if they witnessed us *working hard* at being a great parent?

"You can't get much done in
life if you only work on the
days when you feel good."
Jerry West

– *Shake it off.* Falling down, mistakes, and failure are all a part of life and learning. The true battle is not in the falling, it's in managing the messages in our head after we fall. Pundits encourage us to get up, and that is a good thing. But, we won't be able to get up repeatedly, and we won't be able to learn to prevent it the next time if we wrongly conclude after we stumble: "I'm no good, I'll never get it. I'm not cut out for this. I should do something else!" These damaging words must be eradicated. This defeatist mentality must be conquered. New messages, new ways of framing failure must be developed in order for an athlete to mature and grow. The same is true with sports parenting. It is certain that we will make mistakes, that is not the question. The question is how we will respond to these mishaps. Which messages will we allow to define us and which ones will allow us to move forward? Might our kids bounce back faster and live lighter if they witnessed us *letting go of our own mistakes quickly and completely*?

"Never give up! Failure and rejection are only the first steps to succeeding."
Jim Valvano

What would it look like if we shut our mouths, lead by example, and lived out the principles that we are often talking about? If you want to be a great sports parent and raise a child who will be successful both inside and outside of the Arena, live the life you want them to live!

"We all obsess about what we are doing and accomplishing. What if we simply made the way we live our lives our accomplishments?"

Maria Shriver

4

I promise to always be here for you.

"The willingness to show up changes us.
It makes us a little braver each time."
Brene Brown

I often share motivational quotes with my teams and my own children. Most of the time I gravitate to the weighty words of those who have gone before me. One day, I looked deeply into the eyes of one of my daughters and imparted these words, "I may not win, but I will never give up."

Curious, my daughter inquired, "Who said that, Daddy?"

I simply smiled and proudly declared, "I did, sweetie."

Research indicates that the number one fear for a man is a fear of *failure*. The number one fear for a woman is being *abandoned*. Both of these fears may be alleviated for our kids, regardless of gender, when they know that we are in their corner – and always will be. So the question arises: What does "being there" look like for your young athlete?

– *We need to be there for our young athletes –* ***PHYSICALLY***. My daughter once told me that she almost cried when she hadn't been playing well, glanced over to check on my reaction, and my chair was empty. In my world, "I had to go for a walk." I thought I was making a good choice by vacating my chair. But, in doing so, my absence unintentionally shouted a powerful message to my daughter, "My support of you is conditional!" I thought it was best for me to catch my breath, gain some perspective and go for a walk. It wasn't. In her world, I was abandoning her. Sadly, our physical absence can communicate to our kids that we won't be there for them. This may not be true, but this may be their interpretation. The ability to stay present, physically, will proclaim loudly to your young athlete that you are in their corner!

> *"You can pretend to care, but you can't pretend to show up."*
> George L. Bell

– *We need to be there for our young athletes –* **MENTALLY**. We do this by helping our children to form the correct mindset towards life and competition. Carol Dweck pointed out that there are four crucial cornerstones for thinking in a way that can lead us and our young athletes towards success. She communicated that we need to master the ability to:

- o Be intrigued by mistakes.
- o Love challenges.
- o Enjoy effort.
- o Keep learning.

If we live out these principles, if we teach, remind, and encourage our children to adopt this type of mindset, we will be giving our children a great gift!

"We like to think of our champions and idols as superheroes who were born different from us. We don't like to think of them as relatively ordinary people who made themselves extraordinary."
Carol Dweck

- *We need to be there for our young athletes –* **EMOTIONALLY.** Emotions are a powerful tool in life, parenting, and sports. Often ignored, emotions are typically a foundational source of both slumps and success. A healthy, emotionally safe environment is crucial for growth and development. Parents and athletes alike thrive when they are released to be themselves and freed to make mistakes. Being emotionally present for your athlete means asking questions about their feelings and experiences while being empathetic and supportive. Support your young athlete's emotions and you will be giving them the key to great success in their life and athletics.

Q: *When your child looks to the sidelines, what will they see?* Research out of Harvard indicates that those who live the longest, most fulfilled lives are those who know that someone will be there for them when they really need them. Can your child count on you to be there for them? Can you promise to be available for your child physically, mentally, and emotionally? If so, your young athlete will be well down the road towards success!

"Success is not final, failure is not fatal;
it is the courage to continue that counts."
Winston Churchill

5

I promise to be patient with you

"The key to everything is patience.
You get the chicken by hatching
the egg, not by smashing it."
Arnold H. Glasow

"Arrrgggghhhhh!" my daughter would bellow like Charlie Brown.

So intense, under the pressure of me, a "tiger dad" of sorts, my daughter would get frustrated and be tempted to give up when trying to accomplish something very difficult. Now where do you think she got that from? *Gulp.*

I would try to gently remind her, "Sweetie, frustration won't help. Relax and focus." She would calm herself, refocus, and continue to train her mind and muscles to do what her sport required of her.

It is a good thing that we teach our young athletes to work hard and be patient. What would it look like if we applied the patience principles to ourselves? How well are we training ourselves to persevere on the journey of raising a young athlete? How much work are we willing to put in towards the development of a great kid?

Recently a father shared a very sad sentiment, "I'm giving up on my kid. They just don't like me or want to be with me anymore." Hearing those words broke my heart. As I've struggled with learning to be patient, here are three very important lessons I have learned:

– ***Expectations** are a big part of the patience problem.* Sports Psychologist Patrick Cohn shared his observation about expectations, "Here is my conclusion after working with thousands of athletes: strict or high expectations can undermine and suck the life out of confidence." Regardless of where they come from, expectations are a troublesome reality that require attention. As parents we can expect there to be a high amount of effort at the things that *our children* have declared are important to them. For the great sports parent, expectations flow from the uniqueness of the child, their circumstances, and their own passions and desires.

"I'm not in this world to live up to your expectations and you're not in this world to live up to mine."
Bruce Lee

- *Even the best journey is* ***messy***. One of our family mottos is, "Life doesn't have to be perfect to be wonderful." That concept resonates with me because it frees us from the tyranny of perfectionism. It boldly declares that mistakes are part of learning and it's okay to be in process. Top leaders in their fields anticipate speed bumps and are therefore not thrown off their game when they arise. Successful parents and athletes have discovered that tension is a part of a healthy, normal life – and that tension is okay. Have you given your children, their coach, other parents, and yourself the room to be human – and the permission to be a little messy? Life, people, and young athletes don't have to be perfect to be wonderful.

"Relationships are like a jacaranda tree – beautiful and messy."
Sophia L. Morris

- ***Fruit** may not be immediate or visible.* In both athletics and in parenting, diligence and perseverance have a payoff. The reward of hard work as a parent and making great choices to raise a great child may not always be seen immediately and may not be apparent at all. Maybe the fruit of hard work will show up in a month, in a year, or in the character your child will be living out in their future. Did you know that avocado trees take at least 5 years to bear fruit? Dwarf apple trees can take from 6-10 years and pear trees can take from 6-12 years to bear fruit! I have a phrase I use often in my parenting and coaching: "Somehow, somewhere – hard work will pay off!" How long are you willing to *work for* and *wait for* the fruit of your continued encouragement and patient instruction to sprout and grow in the heart, soul, and mind of your young athlete?

"A tree is known by its fruit; a man by his deeds. A good deed is never lost; he

who sows courtesy reaps friendship, and
he who plants kindness gathers love."
Saint Basil

Sometimes I challenge my children to work hard at their difficult journey as I strive diligently towards mine. I will say to them, "How about you work hard on the field and I'll work hard at being a good parent on the sidelines?" FACT: In the scope of life, what we do as parents on the sidelines will have a far greater impact upon our child than what they do in the Arena. Mere words from our mouths won't bring life, healing, and inspiration – only healthy relationships can do that!

"Be not angry that you cannot make
others as you wish them to be, since you
cannot make yourself as you wish to be."
Thomas A. Kempis

6

I promise to prepare you for the road (not the road for you).

"I hear and I forget. I see and I remember. I do and I understand."
Confucius

"What should I do to get ready for the big game this weekend?" is a welcome question to the ears of many parents of young athletes. Most of us have unsolicited advice oozing out of us, and when welcomed, the advice is shared like it's coming from a fire hydrant. Let's change the scenario. How would you feel if your adult, out-of-college child would call you and ask you if they should go on a run or not? I'm hoping that you would imagine a very awkward conversation with that child. Research indicates that if parents step in and shield their child from normal (non-abusive) situational and relational challenges, we will actually dwarf their development. Shortcuts short-circuit our children's development.

Q: *When do we step in and guide/control and when do we allow our children to make decisions and experience the fruit of those choices?* As responsible parents, one of our goals should be to raise good, competent, and independent adults. Here are three steps that will help you empower your child and infuse their lives with the right amount of responsibility:

- *Invite their* ***input*** *on big and small decisions.* Selecting sports to be involved in, teams to compete with, and which coaches to play for are all decisions in which your young athletes should eventually take part. Passing on responsibility to our kids should grow as our kids do. When our kids are younger, we need to make more decisions for them. As they get older, we help them to make their own decisions. Part of supporting a young athlete is helping them learn how to make good decisions, eventually becoming like a loving life coach for your kids.

'The 4 C's of parenting. When our children are young we use Control as the way we deal with our kids. As they grow older, we eventually become like a Coach. Eventually, we transition to the role of a Consultant. And ultimately, the only influence we will have over our teenagers is Cash!"
Tim Smith

– *Equip them with great* ***questions*** *to ask.* Before our children can make good decisions, they need to ask good questions. Questions allow for the development of critical thinking, essential for a successful life inside and outside of the Arena. As we help our young athletes identify the right questions that need to be asked, they grow in this skill. We need to create the space to consider the question, "What questions need to be asked here in order to make a good decision?" This opens the door for gaining wisdom and learning how to create the grid that will be used to make good decisions. We can continue to help them learn how to give weight or priority to the different competing values. For example, as your child gets older, give them a say in the team they play on. Help them think through the situation with questions like: What is most important to you between developing as a player and being with your friends? Would you rather play less for a better team or vice versa? What is more important in development, the coach or the competitive environment? How are you going to weigh what is most important to you? The right questions are pivotal in making great decisions and living a great life.

"You can tell whether a man
is clever by his answers.
You can tell whether a man is
wise by his questions."
Naguib Mahfouz

– *Clarify your* ***role.*** The structure of responsibility and expectations is crucial in having relational clarity in every relationship we have, including our journey as parents. During my research, I interviewed one parent of an elite athlete and asked them if they ever got stressed as a parent. This parent simply smiled and said a polite, "No." Because of my personal stress levels during competition, I was curious and further inquired as to why there was no stress and this parent said, "My job is to make sure he has food and water. The rest is up to him." It's important to confidently settle on the blanks in this statement:

- I am responsible for ____________________.
- You are responsible for __________________.

Clear expectations regarding the parent's responsibility and the athlete's responsibility enables the child to be better prepared for life inside and outside of the Arena.

Q: *Are you "doing it" for your child or helping them to learn the lessons that will lead them towards a great life?* Research has discovered that when you "over do" for your child, you may unintentionally create the very thing you are trying to help them avoid. For example, if you try to teach your athlete responsibility by constantly reminding them what they need to bring, when they need to be somewhere, and what they need to do to be prepared, dependence (versus responsibility) will be created, and undo the very thing you were trying to build. Remember, one of the best things you can do for your young athlete is to equip them with the tools necessary to succeed inside and outside of the Arena. Are you preparing the road for your child or preparing your child for the road?

"The only person you are destined to become is the person you decide to be."
Ralph Waldo Emerson

7

I promise to have a better definition of "Win"

"Just win, baby."
Al Davis

Knowing that I have struggled with my attitude, emotions, and unfortunately sometimes my behavior on the sidelines of the Arena, I asked my daughter for her help. We were driving to a tournament for her sister and I told her, "I need your help. I need you to help me define the win. My focus can't be on *winning the game* – I'm not playing and can't influence the outcome. My goal can't be to help your sister *play her best* – I'm not in control of that either. My aim can't be to get her lots of *playing time* – I don't have a voice in that conversation. So what is my "win" this weekend?"

It didn't take her long to smile and share these simple but powerful words, **"A win is a positive, good attitude."** As soon as those words hit my ears, they dropped into my soul. I knew that I had my north star, I had the "win" that I could control and run towards with clarity and certainty.

An objective, healthy, outside perspective is frequently necessary to help in forming a proper definition of a win. If our ego is running our dictionary, our definition of "win" will be warped and waning. In quiet moments of sanity, most of us can come up with a "best" that includes more than just feeding our own ego or emotional needs. "Win," properly defined by the deepest, truest parts of ourselves will include what is best for our child in the long run, the other parents, the other participants, and the world in general. In what is it most important to win? What brings you joy?

"Winning isn't everything,
it's the only thing."
Vince Lombardi (the first day
of the 1959 training camp)

Sometimes we forget to define simple, powerful words: ones like the word "win." Is Vince Lombardi correct? Is winning the only thing? Don't get me wrong, Lombardi was coaching professional athletes and was a master at helping them play as a team rather than pursue individual glory. The problem is that this overemphasis on the victory has insidiously trickled down into our youth sports. And so the question arises: how do we hold on to what is good, true, and challenging in a culture that shouts lies? There are many voices vying for the attention of your heart and mind. What is a proper definition of "win"?

- *A "win" is more concerned with* ***character*** *than applause.* For some reason, our hearts and souls seem to crave attention and applause. The fact that someone may have noticed and appreciated our efforts as an intentional and thoughtful parent of a child in the Arena seems to lift us. My daughter encouraged and supported a teammate after they had a difficult experience in the Arena. Her teammate's mother, with a heart full of gratitude, shared with us later, "My daughter told me after the match that your daughter was the only one there for her." My heart was doing flips on the inside. My daughter had played a good game, and with that I was pleased. But when I heard that she had the sensitivity and the strength to notice and encourage a teammate, I was ecstatic! If you want to be a great sports parent and raise a great athlete, work diligently to model and build their character.

"Character is the real foundation
of all worthwhile success."
John Hays Hammond

- A *"win" celebrates* **choices** *over outcomes.* One of my daughters shared a wise insight after a hard-fought battle in the Arena. "Sports are like a progress report on who we really are. The process of the competition itself is like a snapshot of the character we have, the good choices we make, and the ones that we need to be better at making." Research indicates that our behavior flows from our emotions, which flow from our thoughts.

  Since the thought life of the athlete is crucial for health, vibrancy, and success, helping your young athletes to mentally focus on and celebrate their good choices, both inside and outside of the Arena, will enable them to perform better and at a higher level of enjoyment. One of the best questions you can ask your young athlete after competition is, "What good choices did you make out there today?" Over time, great choices will produce winning outcomes.

> *"I am not the product of*
> *my circumstances. I am the*
> *product of my decisions."*
> Stephen Covey

– *A true "win" teaches athletes to become* ***perpetual learners***. Research indicates that those who develop a value of learning and growing will end up with better lives and relationships. As parents of athletes, teaching our children how to learn from situations, both good and bad, will equip them for life. If, on a team or in a family, a culture is developed that makes it acceptable to make mistakes and fail, it will become safe to experiment and be curious about mistakes. If perfection is demanded and mistakes are intolerable, kids will shrink back, not do their best and eventually, they may lose hope. Making mistakes and "failures" normal, local, temporary, and necessary for growth and development will equip your child for a great and successful life and athletic career. Failing and learning is a win in the growth of our children.

"I do not lose. I either win or learn."
Nelson Mandela

Hall of Fame football coach Chuck Knoll once said, "A life of frustration is inevitable for any coach whose main enjoyment is winning." The same is true for the parents of athletes. Frustration is the guaranteed fruit of a "just win, baby" mentality. The ability to embrace the big picture of life, understanding it's length and purpose, will enable you to function as the great sports parent you were designed to be!

"Show class, have pride, and
display character. If you do,
winning takes care of itself."
Paul "Bear" Bryant

8

I promise to do my part regardless of your performance.

"Running taught me valuable lessons. In cross-country competition, training counted more than intrinsic ability, and I could compensate for a lack of natural aptitude with diligence and discipline. I applied this in everything I did."
Nelson Mandela

"If your child was in a burning building, would you run in and get him?" The speaker at a conference asked what I thought was a juvenile question and an absurd waste of time. *Of course I would! 99.9% of the population would!* I thought to myself. The speaker continued, "Would you run into that burning building if you had told your child not to go in to that building?" Zooikes! My heart skipped a beat. There was pause in my response. That slight delay in response revealed the conditional nature of my love for my children. How absurd is it that I might pause to rush into a burning building to save my child, just because I told them not to go in there? I don't know why this surprised me. I've been functioning this way for years on the sidelines of the Arena. This illustration highlighted for me how I would invest in my young athlete commensurate with their investment. They play well; we are all happy. They don't play well, and dad is quiet and unengaged. Worse yet, if they play poorly – Dad might just ruin our weekend! Again!

Be encouraged! It doesn't have to be this way! Children and adolescents typically operate with a "tit for tat" operating system. If you bonk me, I'll bonk you. As we grow older and mature, we are *supposed* to develop the ability to contain our struggles and not pass them on to those around us. Sadly, far too many parents feel injured by their underperforming athletes, and in turn, they make their athletes' lives miserable so they can experience the same misery.

– *Discover sports parenting* **best practices**. If we are going to do "our part," we have to seek out the best way to parent our young athletes. Through reading, research, or just watching healthy parents on the sidelines, we need to know what healthy love and support looks like on the sidelines of the Arena. If you want to support your young athlete without conditions or strings, open your eyes and watch the parents on the sidelines. Look for those who cheer for the other players in the Arena, who don't disengage when their child is having an off day, who don't yell at their child, "Get going!" or who smile and hug their child after the competition regardless of the way they've played. Passing respect and encouragement on to your children will allow them to flourish in their life and in their sports. One of the best ways to demonstrate and live out respect in a relationship is to seek forgiveness when we have made a mistake.

"I believe the time we really look big
in a child's eyes is when we go to them
and apologize for our mistakes and say,
'I was wrong. Will you forgive me?'"
Kevin Leman

- *Commit to* ***controlling your emotions***. Like a runaway freight train, many parents of athletes have a very difficult time regulating their emotions and not allowing those emotions to determine their behavior. Parents on the sidelines of the Arena do and say things they never would in moments of mental clarity. Why? Their emotions are running the show. Functioning as a healthy adult means not allowing our youthful emotions to control us. Unconditional support of our young athletes involves acquiring the ability to identify our feelings, the source of those troubling and powerful emotions, and learn how to control them by managing the messages they are creating. If athletes at the pinnacle of their game require emotional regulation, doesn't it make sense that parents would need to learn that as well?

"I have made a pact with my tongue, not
to speak when my heart is disturbed."
St. Francis de Sales

- *Make a* ***covenant****, not a contract.* Contracts are conditional. If you do this, I will do that. Sociologists call this the commodification of relationships. I will give you my best as long as it comes at an acceptable cost. Sadly, many parents operate with social contracts with their children. "I'm in your corner (as long as you like me, and as long as you make me proud). I'm going to give you my best (as long as you do what I want you to do)." Covenants are much different than that. Contracts are tied to others' performance; covenants are bound to something non-circumstantial, to something higher, to timeless principles. A covenant boldly declares that regardless of the circumstances, I will do my best, "my part." These *10 Promises of a Great Sports Parent* represent a covenant, a lasting promise which will bind you to your child and what is best for them throughout their life. How much more will your young athletes feel free to perform if there is no end to the attention you will give them, the affection you have for them, and the support you will show them?

"Love is not affectionate feeling, but a steady wish for the loved person's ultimate good as far as it can be obtained."
C.S. Lewis

Practice. Practice. Practice. Muscle memory is crucial

for sports and for parenting. Athletes require hours of practice to train muscles to do what they should, when they should. Parents need to have the same dedication to training up mental and emotional muscles that will allow them to remain committed and to respond appropriately to their young athletes, regardless of their performance!

"Affirming words from moms and dads
are like light switches. Speak a word
of affirmation at the right moment in
a child's life and it's like lighting up
a whole roomful of possibilities."
Gary Smalley

9

I promise to always love you. (Love isn't conditional)

"Children don't just need to know
they are loved; they need to know
that nothing they will do will change
the fact that they are loved."
Alfie Kohn

Sadly, love in our culture is often conditional: "I'd love you more if you were thinner," or "I'd love you more if you were smarter," or "I'd love you more if you were richer." If our physical appearance, wealth, status, circumstances, or anything else changes the love someone has for us – love it is not. Love by nature is others-centered, needs nothing, and is unalterable. If changes in your child's athletic performance modify your love for them – love it is not. Through my years of thinking, praying, and writing in my journal about my struggles as a crazy sports parent, I have come to realize that all I really want is to be loved. A sense of acceptance, belonging, and the feeling that one is home is what most of us are really pursuing. The desire for love isn't the problem – the problem is looking for our children to provide us with the love we crave.

Here are a few helpful nuggets about love to set your young athlete up for success in life and in sports.

- *Love **accepts** your child as they are.* The textbook definition of "acceptance" is to take or receive something that is offered; to have a favorable reception of or approval. Loving our children as they are means to receive them as a gift, and to have a favorable reception of them as a person. There are two reasons acceptance is difficult. First, our child is different from us. Regardless of the relationship, sometimes we have a hard time accepting people if they are different from us. Secondly, our child is similar to us. We see parts of ourselves that we both like and dislike in them and in ourselves. It is that similarity which can breed tension in our relationship. The heart of acceptance is to love our kids as they are, how they are, and to help them to be the best they can be. If we focus on their behavior, both of us will lose. Your child isn't as good as their best day in the Arena nor as bad as their worst performance. If we maintain a focus on loving and supporting *THEM* as a person apart from their behavior, we will unlock the door for them to thrive as an athlete while living out great character and experiencing meaningful relationships.

"The beginning of love is to let those we love be perfectly themselves, and not to twist them to fit our own image. Otherwise we love only the reflection of ourselves we find in them."
Thomas Merton

– *Love leads with* ***empathy***. "What would you have wanted when you were a kid?" My wife asked me this challenging question just after I had mishandled the relationship with my child following a disappointing competition. My emotional energy rose and I gave a strong verbal accounting of everything I was doing for my child, "I would want my dad to send me to privates, help me to shape the right mindset, remind me to hydrate, and teach me about nutrition and how to make the most of my opportunities!" She cocked her head and raised her eyebrows, "Really?" My blood began to boil. It's never a good idea to poke the bear when he's already amped up. Upon further reflection – actually a few days later – I thought differently, more deeply and more accurately about my answer. I realized that what I really wanted as a child was to be understood and to be loved in the core of my being. That's probably why I began playing organized sports when I was four and a half. Most of us crave love and strive to be deemed lovable through our behavior. Unfortunately, few of us have discovered the true source of a love that satisfies. This leaves us wandering down a broken road of "looking for love in all the wrong places," to quote an old school classic song. Where are you looking to be loved? How powerful will our relationship become with our child if we give them permission to feel, express those feelings, and have those feelings met with understanding and empathy?

"We liberate children not by making them work for our love, but by letting them rest in it." Gordon Neufeld

- *Love wills the best for your* **child.** An accurate understanding of love will allow us to love our young athlete in a way that will set them up for success in athletics and in life. What does love need and want? Love requires support and sacrifice. I will not always love you as you *want me* to love you. Love says, "I will do my best to love you as you *need* to be loved." In our culture, love is frequently equated with warm, affectionate feelings. There is a problem with this definition. Sometimes loving and being loved correctly, hurts. Sometimes love is difficult, counterintuitive, requiring hard work and sacrifice.

"To love is to will the good of another."
St. Thomas Aquinas

Tom Brady shared in an interview that, "Football is unconditional love." My first thought when I heard this quote was, "Well, Tom, I think you may have had one too many concussions." But upon further reflection, I realized that he was just experiencing the world's value system. He feels loved because he has performed well, achieved much, and reached the zenith of his sports career. Would he feel the same if he would have been knocked out of football in high school? Is your love for your child constant and unchanging? Are you ready to do your best even when they are not? Are you ready to accept, empathize with, and will the best for your child so they can be the best they can be?

"Love is not only something you
feel, it is something you do."
David Wilkerson

10

I promise to Enjoy the journey.

"Enjoy the little things in life because one day you`ll look back and realize they were the big things."

Kurt Vonnegut

Parenting is a long series of decisions to let go. If you blink, your kids will be crawling, walking, running, driving, out of the house, off to college, and on with their lives. Yet, the life you live today and tomorrow will leave your young athlete with an indelible impression of how life should be lived. Assuming you are like me, somewhat motivated to do better and somewhat regretful of mistakes from the past, learning how to walk through this life with lightness and joy is one of the greatest gifts we can give to our young athletes.

We may bemoan how expensive things are, the craziness of our life's circumstances, or things not working out as we had hoped, but few of us have experienced the atrocities of life in a Nazi concentration camp and lived to tell others about life principles extracted in that chaos. Consider the wisdom that drips from these chilling words from someone who lived through these horrors:

"We who lived the concentration camps can remember the men who walked through the huts comforting others, giving away their last piece of bread. They may have been few in number, but they offer significant proof that everything can be taken from a man but one thing: The last of his freedoms – to choose one's attitude in any given set of circumstances."

Viktor Frankl

Q: *Do you believe the enjoyment of your life is a choice you have control over?*

"Life is a journey that must be traveled
no matter how bad the roads and
accommodations." Oliver Goldsmith

What are the chances your kids will live happier, more joy-filled lives if you do? The promise to enjoy the journey involves resistance on our part – refusing to allow our circumstances to control our joy. Is it possible to find joy, even if your child is a train wreck in the Arena? These 3 principles will enable you to discover more joy in your life.

- *Be* ***grateful.*** Enjoying the journey requires gratitude. Thankfulness has the power to change your heart, relationships, and your world! Few small choices during the course of your day will bring forth such a great, positive impact. Consider the life of Nick Vujicic. Born with no arms and no legs, he had a horrific childhood. People made fun of him, unable to do most of the things we take for granted every single day. He decided that he needed to find a way to be thankful, and that attitude transformed his life. But we have a child who is healthy enough to participate in athletics, driven enough to work at it, and mentally aware enough to enjoy it. For what else do we need to be grateful?

> *"I have the choice to be angry at God for what I don't have, or be thankful for what I do have."*
> Nick Vujicic

– *Live for the right **purpose**.* Good parents live for a purpose bigger than their pleasure. A positive, long-term vision for one's own life, and the life of one's child, will enable greater enjoyment. Living for feelings, immediate success, and quick pay-offs will leave us frustrated and empty. Most of the things we want for our children are out of our control. So, getting the game onto a field where we can play, where we can focus on the areas where we *can* have an influence, is one of the keys to setting your child up for success. Make yourself a purpose statement for your sports parenting that will carry on long after your child stops their athletic participation (Ex: I will be a resource to help you reach your own goals. I will be a supportive and encouraging force in your life no matter what!). Intentionally and wisely moving towards a great purpose is not only in our control, it's one of the few things we *can* control.

"Be intentional and choose to envision a life of significance, possibility, and impact."
Tony Dungy

- *Walk with* ***peace & perspective***. These two companions will bring you a lighter, longer journey to enjoy. If there is no joy in your life, start looking for peace. Joy and peace are connected, and when one is present, the other will be close by. Having a healthy perspective on life, sports, teammates, and raising a great child will enable you to step out of the crazy matrix that many sports parents live in to see life and relationships clearly, in a healthy way with healthy priorities. Peace and perspective are wonderful traveling companions as you are enjoying the journey of life.

"If you take care of the small things, the big things take care of themselves. You can gain more control over your life by paying closer attention to the little things."
Emily Dickinson

Enjoyment, "to infuse with joy," involves decisions of the heart, mind, and soul. If you aren't enjoying your life today, what is the likelihood that will you enjoy it tomorrow? If you aren't enjoying watching your child play in the Arena now, what makes you think you will enjoy it when they are involved in D1 sports? We have the freedom to choose how we will live today! Will you enjoy the journey?

"Optimism is the faith that leads to achievement. Nothing can be done without hope and confidence."
Helen Keller

Where do we go from here?

If you want to be a great sports parent, you need to infuse these 10 Promises into the operating system of your life. Below are some helpful, proven recommendations that will allow you to set your young athlete up for success in sports and in life.

REVIEW these 10 Promises regularly

- *Daily.* Life coaches across the country are paid hundreds and thousands of dollars each month to help people live out what they say is important to them. Do you know what one of the biggest keys to their success is? Research has proven that reviewing what is important every day for 90 days will allow you to retrain your brain and begin to embrace new habits and values. If you really want to bless and set your young athlete up for success, review these promises every day for 90 days.

- *Location reminders.* Also, if you are like me, I need the information handy when it counts the most. I have my phone set to remind me of these

10 Promises every time I get within 600 feet of the practice field. That means every time I drop off or pick up my young athletes, I have a reminder of what is most important and how I can function at my best.

RECITE these 10 Promises.

- *Say them out loud.* Speaking these 10 Promises, out loud, over and over, has a positive programming effect on the brain. Research from the *Journal of Experimental Psychology* discovered something called the "production effect." A list of 10 words were given to the research participants. Five words were reviewed silently and five words were reviewed by actually saying the words out loud. It doesn't take a rocket-scientist to conclude which words were going to be remembered more thoroughly. If you really want to set your young athlete up for success, inside and outside of the Arena, say these promises out loud.

- *Share these promises with a friend.* Research indicates that our ability to retain information increases significantly if we share that information with someone else. Besides, don't you know other parents of athletes that need to hear and live out *The 10 Promises of a Great Sports Parent?*

"Success is no accident. It is hard work, perseverance, learning, studying, sacrifice and most of all, love of what you are doing or learning to do."
Pele

Give others PERMISSION.

Health and growth is an "All Play," where all people are called to be involved in the process. Being our best requires *getting close to* and *leaning on* others who are in the same place, and maybe just a few steps further down the road. Find a group of like-minded people with whom you would like to grow. Give them permission to remind, encourage, and challenge you to be a better person and sports parent.

Rigorously COACH YOURSELF.

If your young athlete learns how to analyze their performance, celebrate what they are doing well, take note of what they need to do better, and make changes to get better – your young athlete will soar! Likewise, as parents, we need to become our own best, strongest, most encouraging and rigorous coach. There are many times in the life of parents when we won't hear from anyone but ourselves the healthy messages that will lead us in the right direction.

REMEMBER the path.

This life and our relationships are a blessed adventure. Regardless of whether you look at life as a puzzle to be solved, a battle to be won, or a journey to be explored, there is an imperfect path you will travel down. This road has bumps, challenges, and switchbacks.

In the words of Kevin Leman, "Don't worry about what you don't have to give to your kids, give them what you've got!" If we are encouraging our young athletes to focus on what they do have and give their best, shouldn't we do the same?

"Did I offer peace today? Did I bring a smile to someone's face? Did I say words of healing? Did I let go of my anger and resentment? Did I forgive? Did I love? These are the real questions. I must trust that the little bit of love that I sow now will bear many fruits, here in this world and the life to come."

Henri Nouwen

Appendix: The 11th Promise

Out of respect for those with differing opinions and worldviews, I have put this section in the Appendix. That said, in my humble opinion, this should be the first and most important promise that a parent should make to their child:

11. I promise to seek a vibrant relationship with God.

"Really? Are you joking? A relationship with God can help me on the sidelines of the Arena?" I've encountered these words and concepts often, from parents and even from my own heart. In desperate moments when I have tried all of the tools and techniques available, and I'm still not in a good place, emotions running the show and fears getting the best of me, I have been reminded of the best and only place to turn is to God! You see, the 10 Promises can set the course for our parenting journey, but a healthy relationship with God is what provides the fuel and power we need to live out these promises.

- **ACCEPTANCE ~** Acceptance is difficult to describe, but we know it when we see and experience it. Conceptually, acceptance joins together two concepts, "agreeing with" and "receiving." There is an approval of someone and then that person is welcomed in. And here is the big question: *Does God accept us?* God is perfect and holy and for us to be brought into His presence, or have a relationship with Him, we had to be made acceptable. Neither our good looks, our good kids, or our good deeds (Isaiah 64) can make us acceptable in God's eyes. And yet Jesus, who lived a perfect life, offered himself as a perfect sacrifice, making us acceptable before God. There is no more wondering if we are "okay" or not. There is no more suspicion about whether we are good enough or not. The bottom line is that we aren't okay, aren't enough, but when we trust in Jesus that allows us to come before God with confidence (Hebrews 4:16). If we experience acceptance and favor before a living and holy God, why would we feel weighted judgment anywhere else? Who else's opinion would really matter? If we enfold acceptance into our operating system, our lives will be full of joy, our souls will be at rest and our young athlete will be freed from the performance treadmill of trying to earn our acceptance. Acceptance is a great gift that we can experience through Jesus and pass on to our young athletes.

> *"At the heart of personality is the need to feel a sense of being lovable without having to qualify for that acceptance."*
> Paul Tournier

- **BELONGING** ~ Research has demonstrated that one word above any other transcends language and culture to globally represent the same concept. That word is *HOME*. Belonging is the sense that we are okay the way we are, that we won't be left alone, and that just being who we are is what we are called to do. Many of us look for belonging through our accomplishments, our possessions, and through our kids. It is the fear of no longer belonging that triggers fears of the future when our young athlete doesn't play up to expectation, make the right team, get recruited by the right school, etc. The belonging we seek can only be found in God. In a healthy relationship with God we may experience the joy of a heart that is at HOME, regardless of where we are physically or what we are doing practically. Tucked between the shouts of joy and the cheers of thankfulness of Psalm 100 are these very important words, "Know that the Lord is God. It is He who made us, and we are His. We are His people, the sheep of His pasture." If we have a healthy relationship with God, we have a belonging that can never be taken away from us again! Where, or to whom, do you belong?

"The sweetest thing in all my life has been the longing — to reach the Mountain, to find the place where all the beauty came from — my country, the place where I ought to have been born. Do you think it all meant nothing, all the longing? The longing for home? For indeed it now feels not like going, but like going back."

C.S. Lewis

– **LOVE** ~ For centuries love has been regarded as the greatest of all virtues. And yet, the definition of that love may be understood by some, but experienced personally by few. As I was writing this chapter, I broke up a fight at a coffee house – with a hug. A military vet with PTSD began yelling and cussing at another person in the coffee house. An overly energetic muscle builder decided to try to silence the vet by force. Nose to nose, inches from each other, with fists clinched, I stepped between the two of them, put my arm around the struggling vet and said, "I'm so sorry for what you've been through. I am so thankful for your service to our country." His shoulders relaxed, his hands opened. I kept holding on to him, repeating the same words. I share this story not to puff myself up – in fact, my wife said that what I did may not have been wise – I share this to demonstrate the power of love. Love is the most powerful force in the universe! It is the only vehicle to experience true healing, genuine connection, and life according to design. The best love of all is found in God. He provided us the proof of His love for us through His Son, Jesus. As for us, we aren't in a physical fight like this example from the coffee house, but we are in quite a predicament because of our broken relationship with God. In order to have a relationship with us, He sent His Son, Jesus, to live the life we should have lived and die the death we should have died. I stepped between two men in a fight. In love, Jesus stepped between us and the Father, hugged us and said, "Believe in me and you will live!" (John 6:29) This love, once experienced, alters our thoughts, values, choices, and relationships. God's love can transform a human heart from selfishness to selflessness, which opens up a new door of care so that we may now, truly seek what is best for others, especially our young athlete!

"This is how we know what love is: Jesus Christ laid down his life for us. And we ought to lay down our lives for our brothers and sisters."
I John 3:16

Q: *How differently would you experience the Arena if you walked in knowing that you belonged and were loved, accepted, and significant?*

Recently I ran into someone I hadn't seen for a while. We met long ago – where else? – in the Arena. Our kids used to play on the same team. We were both excited to see each other. We smiled a mile wide. He put his hand out to shake mine, and I grabbed him with both arms. He is a huge hulk of a man – I felt like I was hugging a bear. We had a pretty good relationship years ago. We had a few good talks about God, our struggles, and then I didn't see him for a few years.

I blurted out, "It's so good to see you! I have been praying for you so much!"

He looked shocked, but it was the good kind of surprise like the one that serves as a reminder that God is looking out for us. He replied, "Your prayers have worked! We decided to quit sports for a while. Cold turkey." I was shocked. This was the "all in" family who would go to the end of the world for their kids and their sports. He continued to tell me the tale, "We took a year off to get our family right – and to get right with God. We went to church, got connected, got healthy, and here we are – better than ever!"

What a blessing those words were to me! Not just the answered prayers, but finding someone who is courageously moving towards the true definition of success for their life, family, and sports! He acknowledged that their journey continues. There are always challenges, but now that their priorities and values are on the right path, things are good.

If you want to get into this type of relationship with God, just ask Him. Simply ask that He would come and be with you, wash away your imperfections and mistakes, and do for you what you couldn't do for yourself. I Corinthians 9:24 says, *"Don't you realize that in a race everyone runs, but only one person gets the prize? Run to win!"* God has called you to win at one of the most important games of all – parenting. Winning for you has nothing to do with sports, and everything to do with connecting well with God and your child. And that will set them up for success, in life and in sports, for all of their days!

"God's definition of what matters
is pretty straightforward.
He measures our lives by how we love."
Francis Chan

Connection Point

Thank you for reading *10 Promises of a Great Sports Parent*. I hope and pray that you will be challenged, inspired and use this book as a tool for growth for years to come.

I'd love to hear from you. Please let me know how I can serve you and the other sports parents in your area. I am available for discussion groups, speaking engagements, seminars, retreats, as well as life and relationship coaching for parents and players.

If you are interested, here is where you can find me:

http://setupforsuccess.org
craig@setupforsuccess.org

I have been blessed to be a blessing. Let me know how I can serve you on your journey towards a great life!

Craig L. Morris